THIS IS THE
NATURE OF ALL OF US

RIBCAGE & FIG LEAF
ECHO CHAMBER & BONE
STARDUST & KEY

you are
powerful.
you are
unpredictable.
you are
poetry.
you can
do and **be**
anything.

RIBCAGE

&

FIG LEAF

in the beginning there was **blood** and **water**, **sweat** and **tears**, a whole lot of **love** to make you. now you are here. **living** and **breathing**. constantly **changing**. **shedding** and **growing**. so full of **promise**. so full of **sunlight**. so full of **magic**. so full of **wonder.** story unwritten. no fruit forbidden. everything in reach- **yours**. now that you can be anything, i hope you **choose you**. because you are the **truest** thing you'll ever know.

if you want proof you are a **blooming symphony**, think of the plants you see, flowers you gift. how their stems conduct water. minerals and food. to support its buds and leaves. think of the **blood** inside your veins. how it does the exact same thing. **carries** cells to fight infection. **forms** clots to prevent blood loss. **transports** oxygen. and more. think of the **softness** of your skin. how it regenerates every 27-28 days- approximate. how you can see the **wildness** in it. it is like a seed. the only thing that survives from a plant that completes its life in one growing season. but the bloom doesn't stop there. it never stops there. open your eyes. you are a **wildflower**.

of all the exceptions
there are in nature,
some plants have thorns,
but   roses   are
not one of them,
you   will   always   be
the greatest one.

---

[1] "Though commonly called "thorns", the sharp growth along the stem of a rose are actually prickles – outgrowths of the epidermis, and non-modified stems."

there are **lifetimes within** you. yours. your ancestors. your parents. chosen and unchosen. their genetic makeup flows through you like stars in the cosmos, asteroids in rings & shattered moons. you are nearly as old as the universe and a **universe** in your own right. how grand it surely is. to live in this life.

of this there is no doubt.
you are so valuable.
nothing else in this world
carries the same spirit of
the one who made us. not
the birds in the sky or the
beasts in the ground or the
fish in the sea or the
creatures of the field.
nothing. nothing that
exists quite like you or me.
we are the **first of the firsts**,
the **last of the lasts**. the
beginning and the end for
the one who Is, who Is to
come, and has come.
higher than all creatures.
and **He** knows every hair
on our head.

what makes you feel **alive** is
often what resets your soul.
hold it close.

this is the premise: it was early July, and the day was hot. the month proving to be one of the hottest in years. on the neighborhood sidewalk was a worm. frying and cackling under the sun like the way water sizzles in a pan on a stove and an innocent drop lands on your fingers causing you to jerk. its body was contorted like the lines kids draw to show waves. trying to move but struggling to survive. not getting far. did you know something could have so much life as it is dying, and do you know that is what i see in you? a **neutron star** that still has **so much to give** even as it is **burning**. what a beautiful irony.

shed.   **grow**.
there is so much
more to you
than you know.

you might not know it yet, but you will **grow** to be just like a **forest**. with every step you take, decision you make, you will learn how much light should penetrate your **crown**: where and when. how much energy you should convert for yourself and exert into others. as long as you have water, you will grow. you will hold the **history** in the **marrow** of your **bones**. and if all you are left with is tree stump after tree stump, just look to the rings & find your **infinity** in the testimony of life.

it lived, it lived, it lived, and isn't that what really counts?

human, creature,
or natural, **you
are not alone**.
to   crumble
underneath our
own weight is the
nature of all of
us. i've learned of
it from glaciers.
i've seen it in the
stars.

just like you, the
universe was born.
and just like you,
there was a day
without a yesterday.
a day without rain.
a day where all your
troubles seemed so
far away. those days
are not far gone.
they are just around
the corner. you are
constantly being
reborn in all the
ways that matter.
look all around
you. you are well on
your way to higher.

write it on your **soul**: you can do all things through **Him** who moves the mountains. for He made us in **His image**. died so we may live. loved us at our best. and when we were full of **sin**.

from the top of your head
to the sole of your foot
you are **covered** in a
blanket so warm. it is
there for you to hold it,
you will never outgrow it,
it implores for you to shed
your tears. it will dry every
one. erase every one. your
worries, your fears, your
screams. it is light as a
feather. you will never be
tethered to nightmares if
you just believe. a
shepherd protects his
sheep, and you are a
lamb. there is nothing
greater than the great,

"I AM".

things we are: a synapse **network**. a **world** uniting. **sinew** and **ligament** tying muscle to bone, bone to bone. **strength**. capable of withstanding tension. **music**; a body with many cords. **water**. **ash** and **dust**-stardust, blood and light, skin oil and salt, **children of God**, a menagerie, bioluminescent, **worthy**, someone's wish, memorable, chosen, 65% oxygen, 18.5% carbon, 9.5% hydrogen, phosphorus, potassium, calcium, sulfur, chlorine, magnesium, sodium, nitrogen, iron, zinc, silicon, gallium, rubidium, strontium, bromine, lead, copper, aluminum, cadmium, cerium, barium, iodine, tin, titanium, boron, selenium, nickel, chromium, manganese, arsenic, lithium, mercury, cesium, molybdenum, germanium, cobalt, antimony, silver, niobium, zirconium, lanthanum, tellurium, yttrium, bismuth, thallium, indium, scandium, tantalum, vanadium, thorium, uranium, samarium, tungsten, beryllium, radium, lutetium, **gold,** voyagers, artists, architects, explorers, anything we want to be and more.

this body is a title page,
and you're the <u>dedication</u>.

once upon a time, and even now, water had memory. it was all there was until land appeared, and it separated from the sky in the heavens. it was all there was until it bustled with life- fish and mammals and plants of every kind. it was all there was until it shaped the mountains and even still before it fell from the sky. it was all there was during flood, disaster. it was all there was until it rested in you.

- you are the **keeper** of memories and a **memory**

we are not so different from the life that surrounds us. the fact that we can find oak **rings** in the tips of our fingers, human lungs in tree **branches**, leaf veins in human blood, and trees in the "tree of life", is concrete evidence to the truth all around us. we are no more **ash** and **dust** than ash is ash and dust is dust. no more **life** than the life we touch. no more **water** than the water that we drink and no more **flesh** than the flesh we eat. but we are **beautiful** but **failing falling stars**, one with the earth as the earth is one with us and for us and in us. and this is where our journey starts.

there is a reason why
we are more **soft tissue**
than bone.

- softness   connects
everything.

behind closed stage doors is
where all the **magic** happens.
it is your mind, and you.
you, and mind. entering
stages of sleep, beginning
circadian rhythm. fulfillment
upon fulfillment with blood
pressure dropping, muscles
relaxing, heart rate slowing,
dreams occurring. the second
place we get closest to loving
is believing.

you are living **proof** of enchantment. of miracles everywhere. think of all the things you don't feel or experience but happen within you again and again and again. like the fact that you are taller in the morning than you are at night because during the day, the cartilage in your bones coarctated and compressed. or the fact that your body gives one nostril a break while the other is active because you favor one to keep the air you breathe wet. or the fact that your muscles will work as hard as they can, without restraint, when your adrenaline is peaked, and you need to add strength to faith. or the fact that the body fights to keep you alive with every ounce of its being, killing cell after cell if need be. in its odd little way, it is all for the betterment of you. you who are a miracle without even having to lift a finger.

i think of you.
thoughts become
all i am, and it
shows.   i   am
glowing.

the Son does nothing of himself but only what He sees the Father doing, and this has been the story for generations. that when we see the good worth having, the good worth doing, we want to have it and emulate it as best we can. we are nothing but **carbon copies, water reflecting, moon shining** with the power of the Sun right across. up above.

head   to   heart.
shoulder to shoulder.
you   are   a   **prayer**
beginning and ending.
in the name of the
Father, Son, Glory Be.
it is up to you to write
the need. and there are
so many ways it can go
when you live in this
beautiful,   fleeting,
promising world.

to make room for new growth,
we must leave so much behind.
think of the story of the
vineyard and the vines. the
branches and the fruit. what
happens when it's pruned. **it**
blooms. it **blooms**.

you might not know
who you'll end up being,
but every tree grows to
have a crown.

how blessed we are that His image can appear to us in so many different loving ways. because though the same **spirit** that exists in you, exists in me, we are not the same. and yet, we are exactly the same. for to one there will be given one **talent**. another, two. another, five. be it creativity or wisdom or discernment. healing, or knowledge. each will be dealt with according to their own purpose. and it doesn't matter which we have or the amount we have. doesn't make us less or more **important**. all that matters is who we are and what we do with that "one wild and precious" knack.

but sometimes we can't do it all. we forget Rome wasn't built in a day. every step we take will bring an ache if we've been climbing long enough never changing pace.

we die the way
we came. with
nothing. naked
and afraid and
alone.

to be **alone** and not lonely
means to recognize you are the
only sail in the ocean for miles,
and yet, on the same waters as
everyone else. somewhere out
there, the waves are still, the
wind is calm, and there is a body
of counterparts. and isn't that
what we are? **one body**, many
parts. one unique body, the
grandest of **arts**. you cannot put
a price on us.

you are no ordinary
vessel. within you is a
wellspring of **love** that
you can feel fortified with,
for once you walk in it,
you can channel it, and it
will never run out as long
as you live.

don't you know what
you will carry one day?
a flowing river of white
to feed generations.
your cargo is precious,
and you too are
precious with it.

this is your identity: that through the holiest of waters you have been **born** anew, **sanctified, made** a new creation. one where you are never far from home, never far as the darkness goes because you have been **grafted** into the heart of our Maker who has sacrificed everything, left us an **inheritance** greater than the one we carry. made us all **daughters** and **sons, brothers** and **sisters** of dawn and the forthcoming light. this is your identity: that you are set apart but never alone, **a part** of something bigger as an ever-growing building of truth and love. this is your identity: that you will always have a **purpose** whether you live it or not.

loved. because
He loved us
first.

before you are skin,
you   are   **bone**.
before you are blood,
you   are   **soul**.
and before you are
theirs,   you   are
yours.

with this as your foundation, you can conquer the world. you can tell a story. you can cement the way you've lived your life and are living your life for others to find that you are like a time capsule. **you are a time capsule**. imagine being the **future** presently because in this moment that is what you are, what you are heading towards, what you are building. you can rewrite history as it is being written. and nobody can stand in your way.

you are a **force of nature
stronger** than gravity.
even if you fall,
you will hold your own
again.

you have eyes to see, ears to hear, a chin to extend to the heavens. arms to lift, hands to pray, knees to kneel & give reverence. lips to smile, lips to kiss, legs to run, legs to dance. a voice to sing, nose to smell, fingers to compose love letters. what more could you want? you already have **everything**.

all the important elements
in this world once existed
in the stars and came to us
in the form of supernovas,
bright and **brilliant** and
hot and ready to be a part
of this earthly life. they
journey and stayed so far
for so long to be right
where you are seeing things
from your eyes. with your
eyes the **window** to the
soul, the universe. made of
matter. resembling those
little strands of fibers. the
core, the explosion, the
shockwave. a **star** in final
form, all at once. what do
you see when you look into
the mirror? i see **heaven** on
earth.

your body animates
that which is already
there. it is your **spirit**
that is the life, and
your cup is always **full**.

you have an affinity for all things because you were **made for all things**. to cultivate it and enjoy its simplicities. reign over it and govern it. you were made for poppy fields and summer air and dragon fruit; dripping and sticky and sweet. you were made for midnight magic, moonlit dances, burning passion. waterfalls, and nature's calls. you were made for milk and honey and more milk and honey. and if you asked the source what you could hold if you wanted it, it would cry, all of it. all of it.

from the day we enter
this world, to the day
we leave it, we are
blessed beyond
immeasurable belief.
no one can take from
what's ours.

- a blessing
overshadowed by its
nature is still a
blessing

hands are not just hands. mouths are not just mouths. feet are not just feet. knees are not just knees. no body part is just a body part. it can change you, but it can also save you. it can change you, and it can also aid you. we know if we put seeds in our hands a bird will perch on our palms and eat. we know if we guide a horse to the river, and tug its reins, it will drink. we know the wind can blow and howl, but without our steering, the ship would sleep. we know a fire can swallow a forest and our tongue is full of flames. we are the **architects** of our own fortune and **destroyers** in the making.

the very act of
inspiration is allowing
a form to breathe into
art, and you do that
every day just by being.
you have never been
more **touching** than
when you show others
how to love you.

your body is fighting
around the clock.
it plays with hands and
leaves you with seconds-
chances upon chances as it
is exposed to things beyond
your wildest imagination.
380 trillion viruses and 10
times the number of
bacteria. some cause illness,
but most simply coexist
with you. isn't it funny how
you don't even realize
something is wrong or
register a **miracle** when it
happens? your body is made
for everything you try to
shield it from.

things you are not: your illness, your thoughts, your worst mistakes. weak, a burden, alone, abandoned, far, easily forgotten, hopeless, damaged, or incomplete. your fears, the darkness, a curse, needy, greedy. the one time you were thoughtless, careless, angry, selfish, harsh. boring, proud, moody, eternally dark. everything they say you are when they put you into a box. the shape your body grows into. your anxiety, compulsiveness, or other diagnoses. you are **so much more**. there's no single word for everything you could be.

caterpillar to chrysalis or cocoon to butterfly or moth, **we are always many things** at once. even when we do not realize the phases that are to come, we are built for change. tooths fall and bones fuse. what starts on four, goes to two, goes to three, ends on zero? we do. we do.

is it really change or
is it nothing more
than becoming what
we were always
destined to become?

more than this, we are **crosses carrying crosses**. the very symbol lives in our anatomy with our collarbone stretching from sea to sea and our spine stretching from Heaven to earth. the wonder in that is this: we are living our death and not dying. we are choosing to let go and let God. we are choosing to be better and remember we are not meant to die. not yet. only meant to surrender. only meant to believe there is a God out there who loves us so much that he sacrificed everything so that we can return to Him in truth and spirit and all our heart.

- "whoever loses their life for my sake will save it"

right now, you exist
within time and space,
but you were always
meant to exist outside of
it. let that sink in. right
now, you exist within
time and space, but you
were always meant to
exist outside of it. what
are we if not **pilgrims**?
what are we if not **exiles**
waiting to return home?

in the deepest parts of our hearts, we are **hungry**, **thirsty**, always **searching** for meaning, purpose, success. we become the very **matter** that consumes us, and we don't even see it. all we know is wants, trades, what's for what's. we forget that sewed into the cloak of this body are pockets full of sunshine, invitations of grace, moments to be still, appreciate the rainbow and the rain. the gold is nice and grand, but we don't need all of that. it doesn't make us better. it doesn't make us saints. it doesn't mean **that** we know best when we are **made in His image**, but we will somehow always be less.

PERFECTLY
IMPERFECT

it is not good for a
man to be alone,
so there was you-
suitable and **worthy**.
not to save from
loneliness, but to
share   this
worldliness   with
another. two **equals**.
both infused with
godliness.   making
up humankind. rib
of rib. flesh and
flesh. joined to form
one body. in this
never-ending cycle of
life.

THEY ARE HALF OF YOUR FOREVER. YOU ARE WHOLE ON YOUR OWN. THEY ARE HALF OF YOUR FOREVER. YOU ARE WHOLE ON YOUR OWN. THEY ARE HALF OF YOUR FOREVER. YOU ARE WHOLE ON YOUR OWN. THEY ARE HALF OF YOUR FOREVER. YOU ARE WHOLE ON YOUR OWN. THEY ARE HALF OF YOUR FOREVER. YOU ARE WHOLE ON YOUR OWN.

strands wound around
each other. reds and
blues   and   greens.
always   replicating
random combinations
of cytosine, thymine,
adenine,   guanine.
linked to a backbone of
alternating   phosphate
and deoxyribose **sugar**.

four chambers of the
heart. four reasons to
love poor and rich. in
unison can the lung
receive oxygen. in
unison can it ebb and
flow to the rest of this
body we call our **home**.
no disparaging. only
welcoming. one
another. with the same
love and openness we
came from.

you are still **you**,
and you **are** still
beautiful, and you
will still bloom no
matter what soil
you're in.

you and i are
farmers at heart
given the same soil
to manifest the
richness of our
souls. there will be
sun. there will be
thorns. there will be
crows. but if we root
ourselves so deeply,
we can overcome
adversity. and make
ourselves a home in
eternity where we
can enjoy the fruits
of our labor and rest
because it was from
rest we came and in
rest we'll end.

the wild has no
place to go but
grow.

to be human is to
nourish, to grow,
to transform, to
love, to burst with
color. to suffer and
rip apart at the
seams. to make way
for new
foundations and
bloom violets from
the violent things.
to make ourselves a
home outside these
growing fragile
bones. to travel to
the ends of the
world. to survive.
sometimes die. but
mostly, to live,
laugh, cry.

it is our nature to move through the world the way we do. to be plagued with anxiety about how the sun will someday meet the sea and dry up every useless thing except a sign on how to find the spirit that we left behind when our dreams were out of reach and there was nothing left to eat except the bones of insecurity and their laughter dressed like meat. it is our nature to move through the world the way we do. as if we are the only friends of failure. as if we do not have what it takes. as if we are only rain and never clear sky, never shine, and never bow. it is our nature to want someone to be proud of us. to earn the love that's already been given. to feel unlovable when we do not. to feel as if we have no meaning or worth, and life would be better off without us. it is our nature to move through the world the way we do, but we do not have to. not when we can move heaven and earth. not when heaven exists inside of us. not when there is a love so big that we can be delivered from all of it. all of it.

and so we look forward
to the next thing and
the next thing and the
next thing and tend to
lose ourselves when
there is no next thing.

does not everything
have its time and place?
does not everything
become **poetry** the
minute it enters into a
space much bigger and
heavenlier than you or
i? is it not poetry; the
mystery of it all? the way
words smuggle their
way into hearts at a time
when it is needed most.
if there is such a thing
as a god, there is, who is
to say then that angels
too do not walk among
us? who is to say we
cannot find them in
our neighbors, our
brothers, and within
ourselves most of all?

you are a body of
repetition and **symmetry**.
two eyes, two hands, two
feet. don't let anyone tell
you you aren't **verse**
wrapped in **poetry**.

the thoracic cage.
the one place we
cannot separate
fact from fiction.
7 true. 3 false. 2
floating. but all
work together to
weave a story. a
story that holds
the   most
important thing
in your body.
your   heart.
wherever you go,
and in all that
you do, get to the
heart.

between   your
ribs is a lifeline
stars   are
jealous of.

harmony: the combination   of simultaneous   parallel narratives, presenting a continuous text. and what   is   more **harmonious** than this? that your ways are the index of your mind, your mind the index of your heart, your heart the index of your will, and your will the reflex of your nature. you are **so many different parts** in one body, and each part has a significant part to play, turn to lead. you are a **four-part choir;** won't you ring in the bells and sing?

you are **love**.
you are **art**.
you don't ask
to make sense.
you ask to be
felt.

you are stuck with this body for life, but every time the body is new. there is a division within us, within you, a **war**, but it only shows you are growing. hours, days, weeks, months, decades, lifetimes. these cells can last from anywhere beginning, ending, and in between. your skin never gets more than five weeks old, **and** your mouth is always primed for healing. your heart and brain cells are forever, but every few days, you get a new stomach lining. but be that as it may, as we grow, we age. not because our cells are old, but because the more times we divide, we get lost in translation. we are only designed to divide a set number of times, but all the while, all the while, we are love, we are loved, we are whole, we are artists, we are **peace**, pieces, and master.

there are so many
infinities shifting inside
us, & still we cry for
stardust.

in some ways, **we are our every age**. we will never lose that innocence, that spark, that quizzicalness. the dreaming, the longing, the wonder. why is the sky blue will become why do i love you. why do i love you will become how can i love you better. we are always building upon invisible Lego toys. playing the same games in dressed up adult faces. one day the legs we use to run will be the legs we use to leap. one day the legs we use to run will be the legs we use to seek. no more running and hiding. only jumping and flying. where we climbed trees, we'll climb peaks and valleys. we are always becoming more than we could dream. seeing over mountains. reaching destiny. what is a scraped knee compared to all the flowers that can bloom from the bleeding? why should i slow down when little me has energy for all of me?

when you can
say **everything**,
and the answer
will be **enough**.

- when they ask
who are you,
really

the weed blooms
because it thinks it is
good. the sunflower
blooms because it
thinks it is good too.
but one is loved, so
chaos ensues. but
both belong in this
one world too.

we   pit   ourselves
against   each   other.
how could we not be
lions?

the human in us,
especially the heart,
can only hold so
much. but oh, can it
hold. can it hold.
because if joy can exist
with suffering and love
can exist with grief,
then light can exist
with darkness and
your still waters can be
deep.

what is numb, except
feeling everything at
once until it amounts
to nothing?

to

1. complain
2. cry when we're yell at
   a. cry when we don't get what we want
      i. want things and want them now
3. lie, cheat, steal
4. justify our actions
5. do what we have to do before we can do what we want to do
6. make sacrifices and hope for the best
7. have ideas of grandeur
   a. (that we worry are delusions)
8. worry
9. talk ourselves out of things we really want
10. talk ourselves into things we don't really want
11. suffer in silence
12. put on a brave face
13. shout into the void
14. make messes
15. and dream with our eyes wide open

we are so much more
like our parents than
we realized. afraid to
end up like them,
resentful. we vow to
never raise our
children like they did,
and maybe once, they
made the same vow
too. but is it so awful
that they did what they
could with the light
that they know? you
turned out alright.
didn't you?

birds that leave their
nest before they can
fly sure do learn to
soar.

as you play, your hands
and fingers will find
the familiarity of the
keys, the ball, the floor
as you cartwheel. it will
find the emptiness
surrounded by gravity.
and soon it will all be
second nature. you
won't be afraid to fail,
to fall. in a world of
firsts, practice makes
perfect. think of how
far you'll come. and
never doubt another
beginning again.

close your eyes.
gently   press.
you'll see stars.
just right there.

surgical utensils, a foam
blue tray, the pen of an
electrified wire loop game.
a circle; hands drawing
closer. closer. Writer's
Cramp - Broken Heart
don't get too close to the
edge. Adam's Apple –
Charley Horse - buzzing
red then darkness.
what a night to view the
stars living in a human
body sky. if you want to
see a **constellation**, get
closer.

what we despise in ourselves we often see in others, and that is where the real work begins. we are born with splinters and beams and the purpose of our selves is to take it out of our own eye before we guide it out of the eyes of others.

and so often we fall into the trap of telling instead of showing, but we are all made with the needles we need, in all the right shapes and sizes, to prick ourselves a cleaner path without that much guidance.

love is the reason
we cry when we let
go.

-    sadness is a
product of love

in the equidistant there is a turning of the tide, a need to hide, a forgetting of how we were-happy- for something more. in the equidistant there is free will, pain, joy, fleetingness because this is not our eternal home. in the equidistant there is looking back, knowing, seeing the only thing you can do is move forward and embrace the consequences of your actions. in the equidistant there is earth.

breaths like yours tell tales.

ECHO CHAMBER

&

BONE

breaths like yours tell tales. they echo and reverberate in your soul like music that you can't quite let go of. it gives you no choice. you must breathe. **you must breathe and repeat the story**. despite the quietness and stillness of it all, those tiny movements, the chest rising, the shoulders lifting, are everything, enough, enchanting. and if something so powerful and quiet can do all these things, it mustn't be anything but good.

how sweet is that sound?
that before you were born,
**you were known, and
loved for who you are**, not
who you could be.
expected or unexpected,
you are miracles upon
miracles.

what it means to be of flesh and ossein is to have bones that fuse over time that you don't notice and skin that falls off that you do. **you are history repeating itself.** an endless cycle of refining, never losing. of doing much and great things with the little you have. you are going to be just grand.

this heart, this cage, these
true, floating, and false
ribs. this mind, this spine,
that connects us to the
divine. call it by name and
remind yourself that **you
are here** and were given
the gift of life today.

because who you are inherently never changes, **your worth never changes**. despite what you do, what you lack, who you love, what you don't do, this is the one truth that will remain. it will remain when you are lonely, when your skin is wrinkled, when the lines on your forehead are deep. it will remain when the hairs on your head are gray, and you don't recognize yourself in the mirror above the kitchen sink. it will remain when darkness becomes you, and even still when light surrounds you. it will remain because **you are worthy**. you have always been worthy.

there is nothing wrong with wanting to be perfect or wanting things to be perfect. even the branches of the vines in the vineyard long to be released if it is no longer serving the one thing it lives on, bearing fruit. so try and try and try. maybe not in this life, but one day, you'll get it right.

maybe this body has stretch marks, maybe this body has scars, maybe this body has bumps and lines and spots. maybe this body is swollen, maybe this body ain't perfect, but **this body is beautiful, resilient, and kind**. maybe this body is nothing you've dreamt it to be, but this body will get you through all the dark times. this body was meant to be loved by the one who carries it.

you were crafted so meticulously that your blood is to bones what honey is to a honeycomb. the latter **are** dry and lifeless, but still **a center of activity**. your bones are strong enough to support you, weightless enough to support motion, abundant enough to protect you, and spacious enough to store fibers. we are too perfectly designed to just happen.

your heart will never
be so stained that it
can't be made clean.
never be so sick that it
can't be made well.
never be so broken
that it can't be made
whole. never be so
damaged that it can't
be **full of love also**.

on your bad days,
you are not hard
to love.

even on your worst
nights, **there are blooms
that will happen in** you.
not because you need the
morning   glory.
but because the morning
glory needs *you*.

there is a place for us. for you. the lame, the outcast, the orphaned, the poor and humbled. there is a vine and fig tree planted just for you, your name written in the stars. and you do not have to be afraid. no one can make you feel inferior without your consent. no one can make you feel small when you were born to be large in the eyes that matter. and **you matter**. how you are made of atoms, and you matter. i promise you with all my heart, you are more important than all the sounds falling around you, telling you, "you are not enough."

no matter what the day
brings, **you are enough**.
no matter what the night
brings, **you are enough**.

perhaps you
don't ever think
about it this way,
but just by
standing, you are
forced to **carry
your own weight**.
and doesn't it feel
like nothing?
which is to say,
doesn't it feel
natural? like
something you've
been doing ever
since you learned
how, simply
because you can.

darling little thing,
**you are a mirror of
light** to those in
perpetual darkness.
a microcosm of the
macrocosm up above
and not here. aware
of itself and its
purpose. in the
world, but not of it.
revel in your exile.
you're on the way
home, dear.

you are not expendable. you **could be** the drop that overflows **the** ocean, the **voice** that echoes in the wind, **the light** that leads someone home, **the compass** for a seeker, **the answer** to a prayer or **a shooting star** for someone's wish. you could be **the sand** that quenches fire, **the oasis** in the desert, **the muse** to a god, **the haven** that saves a life. you could be. you could be. you could be. and just by being one of one, you have already impacted everything.

please don't go searching
for all the world because
darling, you are it. how
you turn over new leaves
like the solstice and
blossom like the spring.
how you become the
green   thumb   for
everything that breathes.
everything you need is
right in front of you and
inside you when you're
looking inward and not
between. love yourself for
love of me. you are most
deserving.

you are not human;
you are **dancer**.
you are **demigod**.
you are **living stone** of
the living Stone.
you are chosen; meant
to live with both feet
outside the world. not
one foot out and one
foot in. you are meant
to live like **kings** and
queens surrendered,
thus sequestered and
free from temptation
and sin. you are meant
to live with the
knowledge that you
will be delivered,
united body and soul
into glory. you are
meant to live unafraid
for you are holy, holy,
holy. so be holy, holy,
holy.

every day you are
echoing motions to live
and not just survive.
before you give up on
your body for
seemingly giving up on
you, recognize all the
things it does to
protect you. remember
the calluses that form
on a ballerina's feet.
and the calluses that
form on a string players
hands. it is the
difference between a
good turn and bad. a
good slide and messy
one. even, controlled
strokes vs.
inconsistent. you are
no different than
them. remember to
look at your hands.
invisible though they
may be, it is there so
**you can do what you
love again and again
and again**. forever.

you. you can. **you** can do anything. you can do anything you put your heart & soul into. you **can** do anything you put your heart & soul into. you can do anything you put your heart & soul into. you can **do** anything you put your heart & soul into. you can do anything you put your heart & soul into. you can do **anything** you put your heart & soul into. you can do anything you put your heart & soul into. **you** can do anything you **put** your heart & soul into. you can do anything you put your heart & soul into. you can do anything you put **your heart & soul** into. you can do anything you put your heart & soul into. you can do anything you put your heart & soul **into**. you can do anything you put your heart & soul into. you can do anything you put your heart & soul into. you can do anything you put your heart & soul into. you can do anything you put your heart & soul into. you can do anything you put your heart & soul into. you can do anything you put your heart & soul into. you can do anything you put your heart & soul into. you can do anything you put your heart & soul into. you can do anything you put your heart & soul into. you can do anything you put your heart & soul into. you can do anything you put your heart & soul into. you can do anything you put your heart & soul into.

you will have your moments
in the sun and in the moon,
and in those moments you'll
be reminded, the ones you
love were there for you all
along.

there is so much magic in you that **you are not a one hit wonder**. the things you stumble upon on accident are waiting for you to tap into it, waiting to be found, waiting to be honed and perfected as best it can. reach for that hanging thread. the silver lining in the clouds of your mind. if a camel can fit through the eye of a needle, then you can enter heaven when you can.

the water into wine
wasn't the real magic.
it was the wine tasting
better.

- you are not done yet

if mustard seeds can
become giant trees,
if drops of rain can
lead to flowing sea,
if tiny sparks can
become forest fires,
if five loaves can
feed a multitude,
then you must
believe that even the
little in you is
**worthy of being
made great** *too.*

you do not need to look too far for a miracle. **miracles are all around you** and in you. waiting for you to have faith and believe. waiting for you to surrender. waiting for you to give and share- talents no matter how little. it is from there they come to life and take shape in your hands. does a seed not sprout into a plant when you give it tender, loving care? does a stunned bird not resume flight after it is given enough time to recover? does not even a prayer, the smallest one, have the potential to save a life? no, you do not need to look too far. not even close, not even a little bit, not even at all.

no matter how
rooted you are,
**you have water at
your fingertips**.
and though you
cannot move, you
can still breathe
life.

one day you'll stop holding on to distant things and see how even the up-close can be beautiful. you'll find love in an always raining city, and where you once hated it, it'll soon become your most favorite thing. you'll forget the cold, the heavy, the heartaches. you'll wonder if it has always been this way. if you denied the magic before you really saw it. you'll fold out of yourself. you'll fold out because **you've always been deserving**, and you'll never fold again.

who others are,
what others do,
won't fill *you*.

the grass is not as green as your mind persistently has you believe. if we know anything from science, it is that looks can be deceiving. the grass reflects green, so our eyes see green, but to every other living thing, it has another hue. and the same can be said of people. we never tell the whole story. we wear masks behind closed doors and host masquerades outside of them. but if we love the life we have, **we'll see the better as best right in front of us**. and we will not be envious or let that type of sin enter into our lives and have hold of us.

be patient. have heart. like
leaves on a stream,
everything will move along.
whether you're down, stuck,
or lost, you have to
remember this. you have to
remember it won't be this
way forever. if you can
believe in the nature of every
other living thing, you can
believe in the nature that
exists between you and me.

-        we will move along

when the light leaves your eyes and returns to the stars, make yourself a constellation and remind yourself, "**you are here, but not for long**."

when you look to the world to say who you should be, you miss who God says you should be. and **who should you be other than who you are** with the peace, love, and joy inside of you, and a kingdom beyond our mind's wildest imagination.

you are anything but empty. have you forgotten the structure of you? your house, its walls, its color. if anything, you are **full**. full of love, full of breaths. full of stars, full of all things new. if ever you are in doubt of the magnificent being you are, find a dark and cloudless night, where the sky is blue and bright, and magic is all around in the prettiest of sights. inhale for four. exhale for six. feel the full breath. no matter how excessive. think of the life you give back to the trees. and know **you were made to breathe intentionally**. how could that be if you were actually empty?

even   in   your
suffering,   **you
have it all**.

- support system

put your hand over your heart. **you are not alone in feeling lonely.** whenever you cannot reconcile knowing and accepting, look all around you and remember everything that beats with a life of its own. remember how it won't exist without support from others. the lone dandelion in the cracks. the moon in the sky. the caterpillar in the grass. the animal in the wild. remember **feelings are only temporary,** and though they feel true, not all are reality. not all are reality. you are never truly lonely. not really.

it is a beautiful thing
that tears are also salt.
**you are healing and
feeling at the same
time**, and so weak is
one thing you are not.

there is the promise of hope, the promise of light for you and me. for **the light in us will never burn out**. will never be fully overtaken. like a total solar eclipse, it is only silhouetted. and slowly and surely its lunar limb will climb and give way to a regalia of light. beads and rings- entirely of diamond. entirely of shine with no roughness around its edges. and **the darkness will fade**. it will fade. like it was never really there at all.

in some ways, a light that flickers alone is brighter than many lights flickering together, but you are not on your own. as hard as it is to believe, **someone out there has a light just like yours**. and once the door is opened and the conversation is had, you will walk together hand in hand and vanquish the black.

you are not for everyone,
but **you are for someone**.
someone will love the
meat on your bones, the
accidental snort in your
laugh, the way you re-
watch your favorite
movies or scenes over and
over again. they will love
the way you curl up in
bed, the freckle on your
cheek, the scar on your
arm, the beauty mark on
your inner thigh. they will
love you just as you are
because for them, you
aren't the sun. you're the
north star.

you are water that doesn't
evaporate. **don't disappear
from your story.**

there is no part of you too small. your pinky provides half your hand strength, your smallest and lightest bone ensures sound waves turn into vibrations, the smallest muscle controls how loud your voice sounds in your head, and protects your inner ear, the smallest organ affects how you sleep or wake up, the hyoid carries the weight of your tongue, and is vital to breathing, swallowing, and speaking, and the smallest vessel connects the arteries and veins that carry blood away and to your heart. all of this to say: **there is no part of you too small**. every part of you is needed. you are the player, the stagehand, the crew, the follow-spot, the prompter, director, the audience looking inward. a one woman, one man show. it cannot be magnificent without all of you. when they say it takes a village, recognize **you are a village too**.

you are the north star,
the heartland, the saving
grace. you give so much
when you are here. **you
are so much when you
are here**.

dark as you are, you are no less **honey**. light as you are, **you are** no less **honey**.

the only thing that stops the constant conflict within a star, the collective gravity of its mass pulling inward, is the pressure of light pushing back. **the strongest forces are soft**. even at the core.

and so, if you think of the stars
that do not fight to stay alive,
you will know death is not the
end, but a powerful awakening
to the true light within. you
would not be afraid or
ashamed to be seen in your
most **vulnerable** state. **the old
become young again**. that is
just the way it is.

your body will not desert you in your hour of need. though your heart beats faster, your airways will become open for easier breathing, and you will make it over this mountain. keep on keeping on. **you have one more step in you** and another after that. believe me.

your fragility does not
mean you are incapable.
built inside you like a plant
is a line of weakness, and
when you reach maturity,
**you will split open and
bear fruit**.

you are talking every day
with your whole being.
of course you are
exhausted. you have
pushed every boundary.
said things you did not
want to say. said things
you did. became things
you didn't want to
become. and became
things you did. **you are
so brave**. to exist in the
same space as your
suffering.

perhaps the palm tree is the greatest example of something that can be imperfect and still grow. if we look at all its parts, the leaf, the crown, the crown-shaft, the inflorescence, the trunk, the scars, and roots, we will see from top to bottom, the surface may be rough or smooth, knobby, armed with sharp spines, and most times it is both or all of the above. from the space between the nodes, it tells us it won't stop growing. despite it all, it will mature. and **live to talk about it**. and isn't it beautiful that the roughness leads to the fruits? it reminds us to embrace all parts of ourselves too.

listen. just listen. listen to the sound of the world waking up or the sound as it falls asleep. listen to the heartbeat of another and feel how their pulse sings. listen to the ground shifting beneath your feet and the universe perfectly aligning. listen to the bird, the air, the ocean. find out what it carries. put your ear to the earth and catch your balance. hearing isn't all its for. **whenever you feel the world spinning, just listen**.

even now, here in this place, **there are angels surrounding you, guiding you, serving you** as they are called to do. and if you listen closely, you can hear them in the trees, the rivers, the skies. and you can feel them in your heart, most times.

one day **peace
won't be a thing
that only exists
when you sleep.**
it'll flow into the
open too.

it is not enough for our hearts to be heavy. **our hearts are already heavy simply from living and breathing and existing** in this world where we are carrying crosses, bloody from nails, reopening wounds before letting them close again and again and again. if anything can lift our spirits, it is remembering who we are at our core. the essence that exists among the chaos: peace, love, and joy. and the ability to transform it into little victories everywhere.

you are expanding.
in the joy, the pain,
and everywhere in-
between.

the world is too big and too vast to remain comfortable, less, and clueless. it took us years to get where we are, but there are so many years left to go. in this grand hall, in this echo-chamber of a dome, there is space for all voices. not just the ones we know and love because they love and know what we do. how can we know the music we want to hear if we never hear it? how can we be open to change if we never embrace it? how can we love one another, as we love ourselves, if we never look each other in the eye, if we never wine and dine as friends and not masters and slaves of each other? **we are the greatest things to happen to this universe**, but we are so blind. if only we could embrace our differences and realize our similarities are so much more than any book of history we learn from, the world would be so much better.

remember who you are,
remember why you're here.
not tombs and ashes, but
redemption and **glory**. not
moon and earth, but **stars**
and **heaven**. you are the
body of God. not just His
image or temple. even when
the world doesn't see it,
remain steadfast. there is a
small gate made for you and
<u>narrow</u> is the path.

your power is that **you know you**.

people will come and go,
move on to better and
brighter things, but it's not
a reflection of you. though
it feels like they are leaving
you, **it is not the end**. you
don't feel your body shed,
but you are still as whole as
you've ever been, and it is
the same here. they were
with you on the journey
when you needed it. they
entered at a point in your
life and exited at another.
they time traveled and left
you behind with the
knowledge that would
shape you into the person
that you were always
destined to become. let
them go, set them free. the
night is still young, and they
were never made to stay.

the moon shifts in phases,
& it is still **whole**.

shedding does not always mean letting go. rather it means forming, unraveling, revealing something new as seen in each instar stage in metamorphic insects. here external wing buds form, and parts that declare their sexual maturity. and **it is the most natural thing. the beginning of becoming**. one door opening as another is closing.

every end is a new beginning. we know this by the way we love, we know this by the way we touch, we know this by the way our skin changes.

- His blood was shed so that we could be reborn

you are daughter or son, wife or husband, mother or father, family, or friend, or both, and thus, many different persons in one body. why let one word define you when **you can be anything and everything**, and live and breathe many different legacies.

one origin, one destiny,
one journey, one story,
one voice, one heart,
one love.

the same gravity that holds the Earth together, causes the tides of oceans, and keeps the sun in orbit, exists around you too. and it can do, and does, so much more for you. it is a signal telling the body to be strong, and it keeps you on the ground, and it teaches you to fight while saying: "don't stop at the moon. not when **there's a whole galaxy in front of you.**"

you have almost the
same amount of
neurons in your
brain as stars in the
Milky Way.
**you could light up
a whole damn sky.**

you began as a protostar gathering mass from your surroundings, and the cloud that bore you under less-than-optimal conditions. like a lover in love, there was gravitational energy, a desire to share all and form something from something. the friction between two bodies pulling closer and closer together, begging nothing to escape, desiring anything but space, turned into a warmth so dense that it traveled throughout the body and settled into the pit below their chest. the miracle begun and **the miracle was you**. warming, warming, forming, rising, becoming. a star. and not just any star. but a main-sequence star. maintaining equilibrium between forces of good and evil/bad.

no matter where you go
in all the world, **there is
no one,** and i mean no
one, **quite like you.**

there is not a part of you that you would not lay down your life for. you have it in you/it is in your blood like the mother rabbits that leave their young at 25 days old because their scents are so much stronger and more susceptible to prey. and how much closer to the sky are you than them. how much more blood travels through your veins. how much spirit, how much life, how much water. **you are made for sacrifice**.

imagine that. **everything you need is with you**, before you, behind you, in you, beneath you, above you, around you, in breadth and length and height, and **His name is Jesus Christ**.

think of your heart
as   stained   glass.
remember   **light
shines through.**

you are so much like the sun.
dynamic, sending out energy
into spaces far and wide. and
though the sun cannot harbor
life, so many lives are lived
because of it, and so many lives
are lived because of you. **you**
who **are sun-kissed** and have
been descended upon by
tongues of flame and spirit.
shine your rays. spread your love.
you're not meant to stay gone.

it has always been **the
love in you** that
makes you feel good
about loving someone
else.

overtime, in a field of tulips, you'll notice the imperfections. the violent streaks of color that you'll still find so beautiful. and if **you can find the beauty** in a most fatal flaw, you can find some in yourself too.

what a life you must have
led in the past. what wars
you must have fought. to
be born with such beauty.

the stars do not move like we do. it has one spot in the sky, fixed to be gazed upon. so the fact that we are here, full of its dust, a gift the night cannot hold, so it does not, and we are able to choose the life for us, is a luxury so grand that we must not take it for granted. we must echo. echo for all the ones that came before us. echo for all the ones who did not have means, or simply did not dream because they were rigid to the times of obedience. **we must echo and echo so loudly that we become the magic others finally believe in**. we must echo. and echo. on.

why do we exhale
the air we breathe
if it is not to **be**
kind?

if this body of sin does not weigh you down, why do you weigh you down? if you want to be forgiven, you can be, **you have already been forgiven**. you will always be a sinner, but you don't have to keep on sinning. the path to holiness is rough, you will fall short a lot, but there is so much grace to be found at the end of the journey that if you just stay the course, you will see how your life can be a testimony to how anyone can become a Saint after persevering that much.

sometimes you can't protect
your heart, but you can save
it.

you do not owe anyone
any part of you that you
do not want to give. the
moon does not apologize
for only showing us one
side and you should not
have to apologize for the
way your face falls when
you keep your head down
and not up towards the
sun.

how simply and utterly confusing it is to live in a world where **your life is your own, but your body is not.** and i guess the question left to ask is why do we say it is the moon's glow when we know it is the Sun's?

everything hot will be cold.
everything lost will be found.
everything young will be old.
and everything old will die.
but like some of earth's most
beautiful flowers, **our spirits
can remain**. we can be reborn
again. in Christ. and what a
thing it is to be reborn. to
have a chance to start all over.
to speak to the hearts of man.
and show them everything we
can.

the way they love you is
much, but you were made
for it.

our ancestors ate manna in the desert, but we have the bread of here and now, the bread that is forever. and we will not go hungry. we will not thirst for more. we will have our fill if we go to the places we must go, pick up our mats and walk, with the reminder in our hearts that **our crosses are not greater than us**.

you are not alone in carrying the pain that you've been given. since **your body is the temple of the Holy Spirit**, there is always someone walking with you, allowing you to realize the power in you that is greater than what you can imagine. you can lift the cross. it is not heavier than you.

what are you so afraid of?
the blood in you is thicker
than   water. **you   can
overcome anything**. you
were born to do so.

you will persist.
**you have always
been peace** in the
form of a flower.

- peace lily

the art of growing takes time.
once you have arisen, you will
rise. and rise and rise. you will
never set. you are not a sun or
a star. **you are a spirit of love**.
and until your last breath, you
will wander far and free, and
experience all the things that
you need to be. so let the love
fill you. keep growing like
you're meant to. say hello to
the clouds and tell them you're
coming to meet them now.

say to yourself this body is temporary. remind yourself this body is temporary. live in it, but remember this ribcage is not the only cage you have. **you have not revealed your true self.** free from the shadow of tears and the valley of death. say to yourself i will not stop until i have found every door, tried every key, and learned not just how to be in this body, but how to be. all that i am meant to be. with no regrets. so when you live and live well, you can greet death like an old friend. and the sirens will trumpet, and the gates will open wide. and God will smile down at you and say, "welcome home my child."

stardust flows in your veins.
we've already turned pain into poetry.

STARDUST
&
KEY

all we have and don't is the
potential promise of a new day.
be soft. be water. be brave.

in the beginning there was nothing you could see but everything that mattered. a foundation of sorts. one of thoughtfulness & love that could weather monsoons, survive earthquakes, **change the world**, and make you feel alive. now that you know the birth of an idea is no simple thing, but requires all the breath you have, i hope you give it. for there's nothing more powerful than the peace, love, and joy that resides behind the soul and the life within your eyes.

how to breathe life into
something   dead:
believe in yourself / **do
not be afraid** / **be
gentle** / **take in your
surroundings** / **persist
/ give it space to
breathe** / **return,
return, return** / **rinse,
and repeat.**

you will not know what you need
until you get a chance to need it,
but lined inside these walls is
everything you've never dreamed
of. everything you deserve. more
than what you expected, but
everything you are made for.
everything you are **made to do** in
this life will answer to you. you
are not the puppet, but the
master. you are not the string,
but the dance.

so this is how a revolution
starts. body part to body part.
the mind says look all around
you and process. but not
without help from the eyes. the
eyes say there is so much to see.
where do i begin? begin right
here the heart says. you are
drawn to something. color in
the lines. what do you see
beyond your mind's eye? there
is so much to touch/feel, carry.
be. is it possible that it is all for
me? reach out, reach out. **put
one foot in front of the other**.
do you smell that on the
horizon? hope.

you were born to be whoever you want to be. born to dream and dream big, born to think for yourself, seek the truth, speak it, teach it, be it. you were born to fail and succeed. lose yourself/find yourself. born to love, born to grieve. born to feel and feel deeply. you were born to lead, born for greatness, born to inherit the earth. you were born with all this life. live it.

when we discover who we really are, we will feel it, we will know it, we will believe it. we will become more human. everything will be second nature. we will love not because we're forced to, but because we're made to. **kindness will seep from us** like sap from a tree, and everyone will receive its sweetness. everyone will be able to turn it into something, immortalize it like bones in amber. we will be walking on water without fear. we will make heaven exist here.

shapeshifter, soul seeker. you have godly limbs of water and fire. of cross and bow. it allows you to reach out with fervor, make signs of miraculous wonder, and cement yourself forever in the eyes of our lover. **lose your life**. **set the world ablaze**. be life and limb, for life and limb, of life and limb. it is the only way.

where there is a need,
there is a soldier.
you have a battle cry in
your heart and a
battleground wherever
you **plant your feet**.
live up to your honor.
wield your sword with
kindness. fight to see
another   day,
another   day,
another   day.

at first, you'll sit at the edge of the pool and contemplate. **work the courage** to dip your toe in the water before you let your feet rest in it. you'll watch other swimmers as you move your ankles around in circles. eventually you'll kick the water just to see how it feels. hands **to** concrete, you'll push up and stand. make your way to the stairs and descend. you'll say, "the water is cold." and then repeat that statement again. but you'll anchor your feet in place and let the water surround your waist. you will **walk again**. movements slow and stiff, but you are walking. and maybe you'll say that's enough for one day or maybe you won't. maybe you'll bend your body over and take your first stroke. but whatever it is you are able to do, step, or leap, thread, or wade, you are doing. and that is the most important thing.

- after the drown

remembering how to live again will take some time, but it is worth the patience because you are worth the wait.

star sailor. heaven navigator. space walker. you can wander looking for life on other planets or you can **breathe new life** into this one. it is getting dark and only you can **light the way**. you have seen the wonders. you have seen the signs. how are you going to spend your life with this beautiful, short, and ephemeral time?

do not be afraid to take
heat or grow slanted.
that is how crystals are
made.

there are places you
will not be able to go,
but i promise you,
where you are is just as
important. you can still
infuse all of you. all
your being. you can
still **be the eyes**, the
ears, the **hands**, the
feet, the **voice**. and
what a voice you have.
do not go quiet.
whenever you are
steered in another
direction, do not go
quiet. there is so much
good to be shared. a
message to be spread. a
love to be had. the best
thing you can do for
yourself is allow
yourself to be present
**and accept where the
wind blows you** so
your kindness can be
sprinkled everywhere.

to go where you've
never gone, you must
love like you've never
loved. like the wildest
rivers, you must
surrender to the
current **and ask
nothing** of the
moment, and just be.
then you will get to
wherever you need to
be.

you have your own map
to **give** to the world,
to the ones you love.
it is shelved on your
fingertips and dares to
ask who will you touch
today, what will you
change today, how will
you be today.

be the change, and the world becomes a garden.

when you think about it,
nothing is really a
coincidence at all.
when you're born, the
boundary formed
between you and your
environment is your
skin. as it is when plants
are beginning to bloom.
thorns, spines, or
prickles; the
modification or
extension of leaves,
roots, stems, buds.
what was it all for?
protection. and my
gosh; **weren't you gifted
with a spine**? it's as if the
Lord knew we would
need a weapon that
blooms on its own.

the rest will figure itself
out, it is your heart
that's important. for it is
not the armor you wear
that determines the
outcome of the battle,
but the weapon you
carry that cannot be
seen, beats inside your
chest, and often beats
for another.

let it **carry love**.

to fall in line. that's
what it feels like to be
women. we seal our
lips, never raise our
voice above a whisper,
sit with our legs closed.
womanhood   was
required   and
playfulness   was
privileged. we became
women long before we
became   girls.   walk,
don't run. sit still, just
smile.   bleed   each
month, but never show
it.   within   every
blossomed woman is a
budding girl, and mine
will know how to **step
out of line**.

you've bit your tongue
for far too long trying
to hold back the words
that got you here.
let it go, set it free.
you are needed
presently.

thank you for
throwing stones.
for now we know
how to **pick up the
pieces**, shatter the
ceilings, and carve
out the paths that
we need to take
too.

one by one by one,
your mind will light up.
your heart will fill with
desire, and you will catch
wind of wanting winds that
once your mind kept hid-
thank you id- as you were
wallowing, groveling, and
grasping in self-pity. things
will manifest. you will **find
what drives you**. you will
be your own rescue as your
instinct kicks in. you will
devote yourself entirely to
something good. look
forward to today.
remember the time you
said not today, not today,
and the present became
tomorrow's yesterday?
make room for the ego. the
super. you are power and
motion, guide and
compass, strength behind
each imperfect imbalance.
take control of your life.
for here you can be
something bigger than you.

life on earth is
one big mystery
and here **you are
at the center of it
all**. love could not
be bigger. that
you have this
freedom to dive
deep into your
core and set off
an endless bounty
of triggers that
will catapult into
a series of events,
**there is no
greater effect
than the being
that you are**.

you are the **salt** of the earth
and **light** of the world.
your story is just
beginning. from the
highest mountain you
have been called to carry
out this mission; to **spread
the good news in
everything you do**;
word, deed/action. to **love
your neighbor as yourself**
and **seek less satisfaction**.

- for what would it profit
you if you lost your soul
to gain the whole world

dance when you clean, sing in the shower, pray when the sun goes down. beauty is what you become when no one is watching.

i want to join in the music
of friends. four rational
people conversing, telling
stories, sharing laughter,
being intimate with each
other with nothing other
than string. i want to **pick
up what they carry**, make
it mine, **add some flavor**,
taste the rhyme. i want to
recognize i did more in
this life than just add to
the fugue a melody of hue
and cry.

-            chamber music

THIS IS THE NATURE OF ALL OF US

it says so much of your soul.
that you want to be like the
moon and sun. for
everything and everyone.
but it is okay to rest.
sometimes you can't be all
the things you dream.
sometimes being the hero
means knowing when to **set
things free**.

take care and take no
more than what you
can carry.

you do not always have
to take what is free, but
what harm would it do
if you accepted this
water right in front of
you? this gift in which
springs of **living water
will flow out of your
heart** in abundance
like the hope you've
always looked for in
others.

one day you'll realize, the very act of trying not to be like your parents is the very act that condemns you to a life of being exactly like them. it is from there you'll learn to **pick the good and discard the bad**. (the only promise you should make yourself is the one where love is all you have) so you'll walk up to the garden, stare down the tallest fruit tree. and instead of saying you want nothing, you'll embrace all it has to leave. it is there for the taking. it will never change what it's born to yield. so you'll stretch out your hand and break the generational curse. take a bite of the good and let the juices flow. the apple can fall too far from the tree. you are living proof that you can change your set-in stone destiny.

it's rare, but if bees are unhappy where they are, they will find a better home. and the birds don't wait for the cold to find an ounce or pound of warmth. and the bears don't wait for a cry to help themselves before a hurt. and the caterpillars don't wait to fly before loving themselves all the more. all of this to say, you don't need to deserve a break in order to take one. you don't need to wait until you're overwhelmed to leave. you don't need to explain yourself before you're ready. and most of all, you don't need to wait for someone to ask if you're okay to say that you're not, because you are afraid of being a worry. **you are a catalyst**. be unashamed. unrelentingly.

i know that all you have to do comes in place of all you want to do, and your mind won't let you rest until you do it, but **where is the fire, and why did you set it**, and won't you blow it out if only just for a little bit?

the world is hard
enough as it is.
**you do not need
to be hard on
yourself too.**

find ways to **fall in love with yourself slowly**. like our sun that takes time to rise and greet everything it touches. not so that others can see the magic in it. but so that it can revel in everything it does. its body is magic. **your body is magic**.

surely if the wind and the clouds and all the things in the sky and below it, the trees, and the ground, can let us know how it feels, then we can drop our guard to let the world know too. we are such sheltered people, but the earth isn't afraid to tremble once in a while and make sure we all know it. and when it does, tremble, we stop and stare and contemplate and say what can we do. we run all the tests we need to run, we can pinpoint when, where, the exact magnitude, and ask how we can continue in a climate when there are issues we can't ignore. we prepare for the worst and hope for the best and stay put until the next time we have to do it all over again. and the least we can do is the same for each other, but we don't. we let things escalate before we work up the courage. we tell lies and say it's okay, but the reality is that it's not. **when was the last time someone asked you who was the person you loved so much, and when was the last time you said it was you?**

when love ages within
you, as it will, the
passionate love you
have grown so
accustomed to will fuse
like childhood bones
into selflessness and
giving. "no longer i, but
them. no longer them,
but me in them." but
oh **what a disservice
you can do** and will do
**to yourself if you
always surrender to
the inherent need to
give the good you
have**, the good you see
in others, merely
because it cannot exist
in you alone.

-        you   are
        important too

**we are made for giving and
we are made for receiving**
that both acts of loving
starts a fire in our being
that we carry out into speak
Lord for your servant is
listening or joining hands
before alms giving or just
joining hands at all and
leaning in and whispering
sweet   nothings   or
complimenting   or   gift
giving or quality time, and
there is so much love that it
means something different
for   everyone.   but   how
beautiful is that? that **we
have the tools to become
some type of universal,
limited, one size does not
fit all, magic.**

when your limbs are an
extension of you, there
is no reason not to be
kind. you can literally
stretch out your hands,
take a step, reach out
toward the sun. **you
can shape the light, be
the light, transform
out of a spark**. you can
become water, fire, air,
flower power. alchemy
in human form.

choose kindness
until you live
kindness.

pause and smell the roses
so deeply that the scent
becomes you and you
bloom in the presence of
thorns and bleed kindness
to yourself and every little
thing for **you are stardust
& key**. your roots will
shine wherever you plant
them.

if you give in to the wonder, you'll notice, **you're not just a rose, you're a compass**, and the sun might go down, and the winds may be strong, but you'll find your way home.

it is very natural to have days when you want nothing to do with the world and everything to do with yourself. to enter into dark rooms to process how **everything is going to be alright**. to submerge yourself in water and hope for silence uninterrupted. to drain and pour and heal as you try to move from darkness to shadows to light.

be it planets or oceans, rocks, or stars, very nearly **everything you encounter in life has matter**. so let it teach you that you can change time and time again, anytime you like, without losing everything about you that made you, you.

you are going to do great things. great things are going to be done in you. i can feel it in my bones. one day, you'll feel it in your bones too. that you have not seen your best years. **you have not even scratched the surface**. there is so much to become, and only you can become it. so when you feel broken, when you feel hopeless, don't forget that you are magic, you can heal from all the tragic, and reveal all of your secrets to the one who's going to need it, and surround yourself with love in the power of believing.

the thing about summits
near a higher peak is that
no matter how isolated,
they are all considered part
of the same mountain. so
go with confidence with
the wind behind your back,
the road in the mountain
pass, and remind yourself
all is we; we are one. **you
are not alone**.

what to do after an
hour of crisis: let go /
let go some more / a
little bit more than that
/ breathe / breathe
again / find it in you to
just relax / pray / pray
for guidance / pray for
healing / pray for
strength / be kind /
open windows / find
the light / forgive /be
hungry / seek
companionship / but
most importantly, and
in sum, **do not
apologize for who** and
what **you** will **become**.

- it is all valid

we cannot be better if we do not feel better. we will yearn to fall into old habits because it is all we know. we will build ourselves up to tear ourselves down and why is it so hard to **embrace the** burning **sun**?

but don't all helianthuses
learn to face the sun as if
they knew all along that
this is what they were
worthy of?

what is it that plagues you?
what ailment rests in your
chest that you feel the
need to sequester and
suppress it at every nook,
turn, and cranny? is love
not a medicine? did it not
save you when you found
it in yourself, and at worst,
when you felt the world
had abandoned you? is it
not magic? the butterflies,
the sweet song that makes
you want to tarry if only
for a little while? is it not
true? that love is the fire
that burns and cauterizes
all wounds? if only you
could **let yourself feel**.
then maybe life at your
hands would be grand,
and you won't do more
harm than good.

the things you hold in your heart, in between your true and false ribs, even when it aches, is up to you. **you have the power** to release and suppress. build up and tear down. forgive and forget. and if you choose to let go, and you should choose to let go, just know that no one blames you for having held on to the hope that a part of them loved you even before it all went awry. that you should not blame yourself for falling.

there are so many
battles, and the pain
just knows more pain,
but **keep going, keep
going, keep going**. the
threshold changes
because you change.

here, wish and will go hand in hand. they are tied to your heart and soul, they border on something happening- a chain reaction, a realization of sorts, and make room for the ache to stop hurting. but wishes are not enough, without one, you are lost. **without faith, works are dead**. without sacrifice, gain is bland.

you are not perfect. you will make mistakes. and the people you love will make mistakes too. what will set you apart from them is your ability to **forgive** because you have forgiveness from the Father in you.

whether you like it or not,
what is done in the dark
will come to light. there is
no place to hide, no space
for fig. there is only room
for growth. the past is
dead   and   gone.
**compassion should be all
you know.**

when   hatred   grows
where flowers should
be, **be the sun**.

why do we not want
things to feel better?
when they say it's not
our fault, why do we
insist on not believing
it? why do we poke
holes   and   makes
excuses and prove our
guilt instead of our
innocence? as if this
world   isn't   hard
enough already. as if
we are not **worthy** of
forgiveness. as if we
have not come so far
from who we were to
be who we are here and
now.

one. just one life you
can change. just one
person **you can** save
with your passion and
your fervor and your
faith. just one person.
one person you can
equip. one person you
can fill with the river
inside of you so that
they can find their own
way to the sea and save
themselves too.

live. the poetry in you
has yet to be a poem.

it is okay to be happy, but happiness is fleeting. it is like an anthill spiraling deep underground with the rest of the world, only for its inhabitants to come up when there is a flood. it is circumstantial. and we are not products of our circumstances. **we are instruments and driving forces**, and the choices we make matter. they matter so much that just one choice can save a life, could be your life, and set the trajectory of your orbit forever.

even now, here in this place of isolation, there is still life in this still life. a canvas waiting to come alive between your brush and whatever you touch. the terrain may be uncharted, but **the world is your oyster**. it knows you are a seeker. and every part of it has been waiting to meet you.

there is always someone waiting in the wings and so, the show goes on. the bees will swarm, a queen will rise, its sisters will die, and the show goes on. rain or shine, the show goes on. lost or found, **the** show goes on. the world does not care who leaves or who remains. the **show** goes on. it must go on. it will spin in a dance so mesmerizing. the show **goes** on. whether or not you grab its hands, the show goes on. do not stop for anything. the show goes **on**. move your feet. the show goes on. the show goes on. the show goes on. so **live** because the show goes on.

you have not lost the magic
of the day or the night. the
music that lulls you to
sleep. with everything you
can muster, follow it.
**make the ordinary
extraordinary**.

from the first, i add to last, and my heart becomes an earth that won't stop beating. lush with green, slowly dying, always spinning with the changing of the tides inside of me. this ribcage has been with me through everything. people come and go, leave their stories, their messes, peaks, and valleys, and while **this treasure** can beat outside of its body, it **chooses me** to call it home. it does not need me, and it chooses me to call it home. no one can take care of it like i. no one knows what it sees in the dark or in the light. no one knows, no one knows, no one knows, but i know, i would never forgive myself if i let this light go.

there is an art to taking
control. it dances
between finding
yourself and losing
yourself and slows into
a need for balance.

it comes down to a
matter of wavelengths.
air matters when you
put something out in
this world, and shorter
lengths are easily
scattered by it. so when
the sun travels to you
in beams, remember
the air it breathed.
remember the light you
see is not the light it
gave. remember to **be
considerate of the
shine in someone else**.
and to **never compare
their set to yours** in all
its brilliance.
remember to breathe it
all in. rise and set in
color. even when it's
heavy. especially when
it's heavy.

you will survive. and one day you won't care where all the pain went. all you'll know is that it is no longer yours.

there is no place beauty cannot grow. doesn't the lotus cling to <u>wild rebellious hope</u> as it drops thousands of seeds as it sprouts and never knows what will become of it or what will be left after its leaves turn brown and it stops producing two-toned flowers. it can wait and wait forever as the pond silts in and dries out, but it is determined to bring forth a new colony. one of resilience and courage and love. it embraces the very mud in which it is planted because it knows nothing else and yet that is enough. oh to hope. to allow it to take hold and fill your spirit. to allow it to spread like a forest fire. to allow it to stretch and cover multitudes for those that do not even have the strength to dream and look forward to a brighter tomorrow. the thing about hope is that it exists without there being a reason for it, and we are all the better because of it since we remain and pray as one. so, hope. **hope like your life depends on it**. hope like the world depends on it. because it does. it does.

have you ever thought
about smiling and just
smiled?

there is so much comfort you can bring to a world in desperate need. it starts with those closest to you. close enough to hear your heart. close enough to feel your impact. even if there is nothing left to say or you do not know what to say, your presence can fill the void of silence that words don't know how to fill. by being there, an active listener offering a shoulder, **you are doing more than you realize**. even if it doesn't feel like enough, i guarantee it is. by praying for someone you love and asking the spirit to guide you on how you can be there for them, **you are doing enough**. and when the time comes when they're nearly completely healed, they'll remember this and say, "you did nothing, but you stayed. that is more than what i can say for the rest."

breathe. sing. breathe. sing. breathe. **sing. until you get where you want**. until you reach the end. until you can begin again.

THIS IS THE NATURE OF ALL OF US

you can do more with your life. **you aren't meant to play the same roles over and over again**. even if you're good at it. even if there's no-one better. you owe it to yourself to try something different. to branch out of comfort. for if you accepted the same things, what would change? if you accepted the same things, when would you grow? there is always more. there is always light in you. the glass is not empty, but full of opportunity. and it is yours for the drinking.

i want to be like the moon that does not rest, the stars that crown the night, the sky in all its vastness, the birds that sing arise, the dawn that announces the second coming, the sun that touches everything, the water that softens everyone and not just me. i want to be the scythe that gathers the harvest and the sheaf that binds it. but most of all, i just want to be **what God wants me to be**. and i want what God wants for me.

do not settle for anything.
until it, whatever it is, stops
weighing so heavy on your
heart.

go after the things you love. you have another heart for this reason. it runs from your knee to your heel and is helpful for walking and sprinting. it functions just like your other heart- even pumping blood to it. it defies gravity.

**you cannot help the
fire in you,** and **you
cannot help the storm.**
fire will always follow
the path of what it
loves, and a storm is
nothing without the
eye and wall cloud.

since the beginning of time, we have been in search of a better quality of life. it was not enough that we had everything. we needed more, we needed to know, we needed to satisfy our curiosity. we have allowed ourselves to become tempted. by a love we do not need. we will drop everything. pick up and move. in search of more love than the love we're used to. we have become a people of convenience. worldly. unholy. justifying greed and other sins to meet us instead of sacrificing it for the greater good of our souls. but the world is not forever. these bodies are not forever. these goods are not forever, and as long as we are His forever, **we owe it to ourselves to be more mindful** of our brevity, our impact, our desire, and how it will shape our future for generations to come.

the work never ends.
as long as you breathe,
the work never ends.
there are always mouths
hanging open, waiting to
be fed. your own, your
dreams, your wounds,
your heart. that of the
world. that of nature.
that of spirit and soul.

the instinct to do something with our life, something good and lasting, is so innately wound in us that **we have always been creators and co-creators biding our time**, leaving something interminable, passing soundwaves until sleep calls us forever.

you are elemental. which is to say, **you possess all five elements**. water. fire. air. earth. and spirit. it is in this spirit you were born; it is in this spirit you will leave. having given life to the trees, having filled the seas, having loved, and lost, having moved mountains, having set sail, having been fishers of men. you have changed the world. you have earned your rest.

in the end there is the leaving of the body that welcomed you into this world. there is ash and dust, pearly gates, and a blare of trumpets. in the end there is who you are, what you've done, and what you've left. in the end there is a sea of chains. broken. **in the end there is a bright light to welcome you home.**

the cocoon is nice, but everyone has to learn to fly sometimes. you've spent your whole life preparing for this. digesting everything in sight so you can get a glimpse of sun in a new body. and though you don't have long as a butterfly, **you are still someone worth believing in**. believe in yourself and fly.

TO HUMANITY. MAY WE REMEMBER WHO WE ARE AT OUR CORE, BE KIND TO OURSELVES, ONE ANOTHER, DO WHAT WE LOVE, AND LOVE WHAT WE DO, AND CHANGE THE WORLD FOR THE BETTER.

HARPER NIGHTINGALE IS A PSEUDO WRITER AND CREATOR SERVING THE WORLD BY FULFILLING HER CALLING AS A CATHOLIC POET AND SINGER. DEEPLY INSPIRED BY NATURE, SHE HOPES TO REMIND OTHERS THAT THEY ARE NOT ALONE BY FINDING THE CORRELATION BETWEEN IT AND HUMANITY. ***THIS IS THE NATURE OF ALL OF US*** IS HER SECOND COLLECTION OF POETRY. VISIT HER AT WWW.HARPERNIGHTINGALE.COM OR @HARPERNIGHTINGALE.

RESOURCES

Depressed

    1 Kings 19:1-9

    Psalm 42:5-11

    Psalm 130

    Isaiah 61:3

Disappointed

    Proverbs 23:18

    Romans 5:4-5

    1 Peter 2:6

Discouraged

    Deuteronomy 31:8

    2 Corinthians 7:6

    Galatians 6:9

    Hebrews 12:5-6

Doubtful

    Matthew 17:14-20

    Luke 7:18-23

    John 20:24-29

    James 1:5-8

Guilt

    Romans 3:21-31

    Romans 8:1-17

    1 John 3:18-24

Hurt

    Isaiah 11:9

    Luke 6:28

    1 Thessalonians 3:1-8

Insecure

    Exodus 3:7-4:17

    Numbers 13:25-30

    1 Peter 4:10-11

Intimidated

    Genesis 15:1

    Psalm 27:1

    Psalm 46:1-3

    Acts 4:31

Jealous

    1 Corinthians 13:4

    James 3:13-18

    1 Peter 2:1

Lonely

    1 Kings 19:1-18

    Psalm 68:6

    John 16:5-15

    Hebrews 10:25

    Hebrews 13:5

SUICIDE & CRISIS HOTLINE: 988

Mourning

2 Samuel 1:1-12
Nehemiah 1:1-11
Psalm 23
Psalm 31:10, 14
John 11:33-35
John 16:33
1 Peter 5:7

Rebellious

1 Samuel 15:22-23
Proverbs 27:12
Titus 1:10

Rejected

Psalm 27:9-10
Psalm 77:1-12
Jeremiah 33:25
Mark 6:1-6

Sad

1 Samuel 1:15-18
Nehemiah 8:10-12
Psalm 42:5-11
Romans 12:15

Stressed

Exodus 18:13-25
Psalm 62:1-8
Matthew 11:28-30
Mark 6:31-32

Tempted

Matthew 4:1-11
Mark 14:38
1 Corinthians 10:13
Hebrews 2:18

Weak

Psalm 73:26
2 Corinthians 12:8-10
2 Corinthians 13:3-4
Philippians 3:21

Worried

Matthew 6:25-34
Luke 10:38-42
Philippians 4:6-9
1 Peter 5:7

YOU ARE NOT ALONE

POEMS, ILLUSTRATIONS, AND COVER DESIGN BY HARPER NIGHTINGALE.

OTHER WORKS:

IN A WORLD WHERE YOU ARE HERE